M000202420

These simple, yet profound, devotions, bring the light and life of scripture to those who are struggling through times of darkness and depression. Philippa writes with raw honesty, gentle humour and, above all, Christ-centred hope. There are treasures here for all of us, however we are feeling.

Vaughan Roberts
Rector of St Ebbe's, Oxford
Director of Proclamation Trust

This is a lovely book. Pastoral, sensitive and full of wisdom, it offers comfort and companionship to those who are struggling. I've been blessed and encouraged by it. I am thankful to Philippa for sharing from her own experiences and for reminding me of the God who shines brightest in the dark.

Emma Scrivener
Blogger at emmascrivener.net
Author of *A New Name* and *A New Day*

These beautiful, honest and hope-filled devotions are a joy to read. With a poet's ear and a pastor's heart, Philippa Wilson gently points bruised believers to the saviour who became bruised for us. I am confident that these devotions will be part of the way God answers the suffering believer's cry, 'Send out your light and truth, let them lead me' (Ps. 43:3) and brings them to himself.

Matt Searles
Director of Training, South Central Gospel Partnership
Author of *Tumbling Sky: Psalm Devotions for Weary Souls*

In the darkest of days, sometimes all we can consume is a few morsels at a time. *A Certain Brightness* provides just that – morsels of gospel truth. This devotional is written for the weary and down-trodden. It is a gentle and quiet whisper that cuts into the cacophony of our minds, reminding us of the One who loves us most.

Christina Fox
Counselor, writer, retreat speaker, and author of *A Heart Set Free: A Journey to Hope Through the Psalms of Lament*

When I first picked up *A Certain Brightness* by Philippa Ruth Wilson and skimmed the table of contents, I immediately knew this would be a book that would bless, encourage, and give hope to everyone who read it. And then, before I had even read a dozen of the super-short chapters, I wanted to make Philippa my friend – that's how warm and winsome she is in her writing. Readers in the midst of hardship – those seasons when it's so taxing to read and process – will especially appreciate how Philippa presents comforting truths from Scripture in five short words. I'm making a list of friends and counselees who will love this book, confident it will help them feel embraced and strengthened by the Father of mercies and the God of all comfort. I'm so grateful the Lord led Philippa to write it.

Janice Cappucci
ACBC Certified Biblical Counselor and author of
Storm Clouds of Blessings: True Stories of Ordinary People Finding Hope and Strength in Times of Trouble

A wonderful and refreshing treat, written out of personal experience of loss and depression. These five-word biblical truths and Philippa's thoughtful meditations provide bite-sized nourishment and encouragement for dark times. A book to be savoured slowly and reread.

John Wyatt
Author of *Matters of Life and Death*

When we feel our most broken, the Word of God can feel overwhelming – big, complex, beautiful and exhausting all at once. So often in these times the temptation is to avoid rather than seek it. By bringing us back to gospel basics with gentleness, passion and poise, *A Certain Brightness* offers the full breadth of God's promises to us in manageable – five word! – chunks that even the most weary can handle. These words of hope will refresh your soul.

Katie Stileman
Publishing Consultant

A Certain Brightness comes as a breath of fresh air in a world of carefully curated social media profiles and their unremittingly upbeat images. Such is the pressure to maintain our public personas that we are rarely honest about the challenges we face in living the Christian life. These reflections show us that we need not despair when we meet with difficulties and disappointments. Rather, Philippa encourages us to lift our eyes off ourselves and fix them on the unchanging character and purposes of God. As we do, we discover that in whatever circumstances we find ourselves Jesus is our comfort, our strength and our hope.

James Griffiths
Vicar, St Denys Church, Cardiff

Philippa has long been a huge encouragement to us as she seeks to fix her eyes on Jesus through the valleys of life. This book helpfully distills profound gospel-centred thoughts into accessible daily devotionals. It will help anyone facing trials and darker seasons of life to cling to Jesus (or rather, and more wonderfully, to see how Jesus clings on to them). We're so grateful this book exists – it was a blessing for us to read, and it will be a helpful resource to pass on to others who need the hope of the gospel to shine into the dark valleys that they pass through.

Scott and Cathy Thomson
Gospel Centred Parenting

When the brokenness of the world feels overwhelming, and we feel as though the darkness is surrounding us, these bite-size, yet Biblically rich, devotions, will help point us back to the saviour who meets us in our brokenness, remind us of the gospel, and encourage us to keep rejoicing in the midst of the darkness. Many of these devotions started life in an online blog, and during my work with UCCF I often found myself recommending them to the students I worked with. I am delighted that this book of devotions will now be available for many more to benefit from.

Charlotte Downing
UCCF Staff Worker (2016-2018)

A
Certain
Brightness

Bible Devotions for Troubled Times

Philippa Ruth Wilson

CHRISTIAN
FOCUS

Scripture, unless otherwise marked, is taken from the *Holy Bible, New International Version*®, NIV® Copyright ©1973, 1978, 1984, 2011 by Biblica, Inc.® Used by permission. All rights reserved worldwide.

Scripture quotations marked esv are taken from *The Holy Bible, English Standard Version*, copyright © 2001 by Crossway Bibles, a publishing ministry of Good News Publishers. Used by permission. All rights reserved. esv Text Edition: 2011.

Scripture quotations marked bsb are taken from *The Berean Bible* (www. Berean.Bible) Berean Study Bible (BSB) © 2016, 2020 by Bible Hub and Berean Bible. Used by Permission. All rights reserved.

Scripture quotations marked kjv are taken from *King James Version*.

Copyright © Philippa Ruth Wilson 2021

hardback ISBN 978-1-5271-0691-8
epub ISBN 978-1-5271-0735-9
mobi ISBN 978-1-5271-0736-6

10 9 8 7 6 5 4 3 2 1

Published in 2021
by
Christian Focus Publications, Ltd.
Geanies House, Fearn,
Ross-shire, IV20 1TW, Scotland.
www.christianfocus.com

Cover design by Daniel Van Straaten

Artwork (cover illustration and internals) by Rebekah Lesan

The Fell Types are digitally reproduced by
Igino Marini. www.iginomarini.com

Printed and bound by Gutenberg, Malta

All rights reserved. No part of this publication may be reproduced, stored in a retrieval system, or transmitted, in any form, by any means, electronic, mechanical, photocopying, recording or otherwise without the prior permission of the publisher or a licence permitting restricted copying. In the U.K. such licences are issued by the Copyright Licensing Agency, 4 Battlebridge Lane, London, SE1 2HX. www.cla.co.uk

CONTENTS

For Timothy, Oliver, Phoebe and Isaac.
May you grow up knowing His brightness.

Introduction

Those who look to him are radiant; their faces are never covered with shame. (Ps. 34:5)

Early on in my Christian life I realized that discipleship wasn't going to be the glorious victory march I had envisaged. I had been a Christian for five years when I was first treated for depression. A year later I was dumped by someone I had thought I might marry. Two years later I went to work for a mission organization in France, but faced a degree of failure in ministry (and communication!) for which I was not prepared. Hang on, I thought, wasn't I supposed to be a gang-converting, nation-changing mother of three by now? Life felt unrelentingly difficult, unrelentingly disappointing.

A few years later, I began to write *A Certain Brightness*. I liked the phrase, 'A Certain Brightness', because it encompassed both the fact that sometimes the bright

Christian life doesn't look how we might expect, and the fact that there is nonetheless a hope of which we can be sure.

Even though in many ways my Christian life did not pan out how I expected, I found that time and time again the Bible bore witness to Jesus. His brightness was certain and steadfast: tenderness for the broken, light for those in darkness. Despite my disappointments, the Bible bore witness to a Redeemer who was more than capable of plumbing my deepest depths and bringing me hope there. The devotions in this collection were written in times of depression, heartbreak and pain. But they are written to point to a trustworthy Saviour, the one who fulfils the promise of Isaiah 42:3, 'A bruised reed he will not break, and a smouldering wick he will not snuff out.'

Each devotion is based on a five-word truth taken from the Bible. The five-word truths come from across the whole of Scripture in order to demonstrate that God's grace, love and kindness to us in Jesus stretch across all time: it turns out that every believer is a bruised one, that we have a God who comes to meet us in our brokenness, and that sometimes He does it five words at a time!

Of course, with five-word segments there is a danger of not sufficiently considering the context or the big picture. In applying the bite-sized Bible verses, I have aimed to explore and understand them in their appropriate contexts. But bearing in mind how hard it can be to concentrate in times of sadness, I've deliberately focussed on five words so that even the most exhausted, energy-deprived person might be able to read and meditate on them, and hopefully meet Jesus in them. Use the five words in the way that best helps you to embrace them: write them on Post-its, create a checklist to memorize them, post calligraphic versions on Instagram; whatever enables you to hold on to the comfort.

At the end of each section there are a few words from a hymn. These serve as a reminder that bruised believers through the ages have found cause to turn their thoughts and prayers to song, and to praise the one who is tender towards His children, even in their darkness. They are also there so that, along with your five words of Scripture, you might get an earworm that embeds truth in your mind or stirs your heart to praise!

My prayer is that as you read these devotions you are able to see and cling to God's goodness, and that even in the darkest seasons you will know Jesus' comfort and light. I pray that you will know Him as a certain brightness in your life.

I WILL SURELY BLESS YOU

GENESIS 22:17

Through the years, there have been things I have asked the Lord to provide: a starring role in the school play, a functioning car, a boyfriend/husband (both specific people and generic ideals, for myself and for friends), salvation for my loved ones, healing for a close friend's terminally ill husband, and more.

For some requests, I can see why God answers no. Given the hash I made of my minor role in *Fantastic Mr Fox* (I lost my shoe on my way to the stage and spent my performance wriggling around trying to hide my naked foot), I am sure He was shielding me from further humiliation.

But some of these unmet desires have left me with questions: Why would God choose to answer this prayer this way? How do I go on asking if God's provision seems so unlikely? How can I echo Abraham's words in Genesis 22:14 with confidence, 'The LORD will provide', when I feel so disappointed? How can I trust God when He says, 'I will surely bless you'?

Abraham knew disappointment. He waited years for a son. He pleaded and wrestled and longed that the Lord would provide, according to His promise. And eventually, his prayer was answered. But it was later in his life when Abraham was deeply convicted: the LORD will provide.

At this time, Abraham was asked to sacrifice the precious son he had waited so long for. When he said, 'God himself will provide the lamb for the burnt offering' (v. 8), he was acknowledging that for Isaac to live a substitute was required. God had to provide.

And He did. God met Abraham's biggest need. A substitute was given, and Abraham saw the truth like never before: on the mountain of the LORD, the LORD will provide.

Years later, on another mountain, the LORD Himself provided again.

If I search for God's provision at the foot of my opening list, I might be tempted to say, 'The Lord withholds!' But when I seek it at the foot of the cross, on the mountain, God's provision is clear. His provision is *abundant*: He does not spare His Beloved. His provision is *complete*: He makes the life of Jesus a sin offering, and His righteousness, His life, and His glory are given to us. His provision is *eternal*: a future and a hope and, in the end, all things. This is the ultimate revelation of the LORD's character. It is the fundamental demonstration of His tender kindness, excessive generosity and sky-high love.

Some of my questions remain unanswered. There is still a struggle with unmet desires. But can I trust God when He promises to bless me?

On the mountain of the LORD, a thousand times, yes!

Generous Lord, thank You so much that in my time of greatest need, You did not withhold anything, but gave me Jesus, as a Saviour and Substitute. Knowing this love, help me trust You with all that my heart longs for. For Jesus' glory, Amen.

To God be the glory, great things He has done!
So loved He the world that He gave us His Son!
Who yielded His life, an atonement for sin
And opened the life-gate that all may go in!
Frances van Alstyne (1820–1915)

GOD MEANT IT FOR GOOD

GENESIS 50:20 (ESV)

These words come as a remarkable conclusion to Genesis. Humanity has chosen rebellion and self-rule over the kind provision of a loving Creator, time and time again, and book one isn't even finished yet. But at the end of Genesis we find Joseph, who has suffered for years under burdens of his own pride, his brothers' jealousy, an adulteress' lust and her husband's fury, looking back on all this and saying, 'God meant it for good'. Joseph, who has endured pits and prisons, heartaches and homelessness, sees the One who is at work in all these things and praises Him for His goodness.

Remarkably, as Joseph was rejected by his brothers, subjected to intense temptation, and then falsely accused, imprisoned and despised, the LORD brought about abundant and overflowing blessing. He worked so that not only Joseph was blessed but his family, Israel, Egypt and the nations too.

Yet even as he said these words, Joseph must have felt the weight of countless years of loneliness, disappointment, perplexity and despair.

Sometimes I look at parts of my own life and the experiences feel like ugly, unnecessary scars that have been burdens and barriers, rather than gateways to any kind of blessing. But when we can't see how God has redeemed yet, these five words offer hope.

Whatever else may have been intended, God intends good. What's more, Joseph's life foreshadows the life of another. In the sufferings and death of the Man of Sorrows, God intended good.

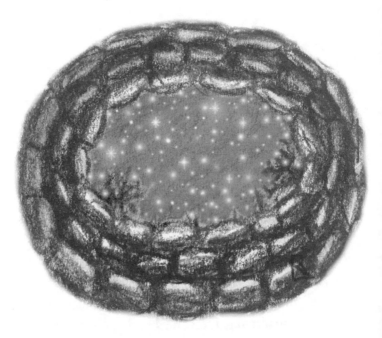

Jesus still bears the marks of His suffering, but now He reigns, enthroned as an everlasting witness to God's power to redeem. He suffered beyond fathoming and, as He did, He brought incomparable blessing to the nations. The scars on Jesus' hands, public and permanent, were inflicted for hatred, for humiliation, for harm. But God meant them for eternal, nation-changing, everlasting good.

May God give us faith in His power to do good in all things.

Sovereign Lord, sometimes it seems impossible that You could work through my painful circumstances for good. Sometimes it seems like evil and harm and heartache are triumphing. Help me today to trust in Your unwavering intention and power to do good. Thank You that You have shown Yourself to be a Redeemer. Help me see more of Jesus, whose immeasurable suffering brought about immeasurable blessings.

> *Judge not the Lord by feeble sense,*
> *But trust Him for His grace,*
> *Behind a frowning providence,*
> *There lies a smiling face:*
> *His purposes will ripen fast,*
> *Unfolding every hour,*
> *The bud may have a bitter taste,*
> *But sweet will be the flower.*
> William Cowper (1731–1800)

UNDERNEATH ARE THE EVERLASTING ARMS

DEUTERONOMY 33:27

When I was 17, I went parasailing. Now, at the time I was suffering from a) depression and b) being a teenager. I was not enjoying the holiday. I was deeply anxious about my sin, I was wrestling with guilt, and I felt frustrated with God.

But I went parasailing anyway.

I was hooked up to a harness and propped on the end of the boat. As the speed increased the parachute billowed and I was lifted up into the glorious blue sky. Soon the boat was a little dot beneath me.

Initially I felt anxious. I could hear the harness creaking and briefly I wondered what might happen if I plummeted into the sea, or if I became unattached and was transported miles through the air, my journey ending with a crash landing in a quiet village on the other side of the island. What an undignified way to die! (Because I was suffering from being a teenager, an undignified death was a far more terrible thought than a painful one!)

But a few minutes later I realized: my worrying would make no difference to my security. It was the harness, the parachute and the tethering on the boat that made the difference. If I trusted the equipment, I'd enjoy the time 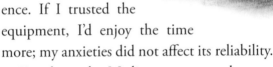 more; my anxieties did not affect its reliability.

Far above the Mediterranean, my heart was filled with peace. And not just about the parasailing, but about the nature of my Father. I realized that my anxieties and guilt did not have any effect on the trustworthiness of God! My feelings could not undo His nature or His promise!

Underneath all of my fears were the rock-solid, unfaltering, everlasting arms. And His covenant faithfulness, rather than my faith, guaranteed it.

Although it was not my trust in the parachute that got me in the air, trusting it did make a difference to my enjoyment. Similarly, trusting Jesus makes a difference to my joy. But even when my trust is wobbly, His utterly faithful commitment to my eternal security does not change: underneath are the everlasting arms.

God my rock, thank You that it is You, not my faith, that keeps me secure. Thank You that when I am anxious and doubt-filled and feel overwhelmed with insecurity, underneath are Your everlasting arms. You will not let me go. Help me to trust in the reality of Your steadfast care. Thank You that in the meantime, whether I feel it or not, You will still hold me secure.

Other arms grow faint and weary,
These can never faint, nor fail;
Others reach our mounts of blessing,
These our lowest loneliest vale.
O that all might know His friendship!
O that all might see His charms!
O that all might have beneath them
Jesus' everlasting arms.
Albert Benjamin Simpson (1843–1914)

I HAVE SEEN YOUR TEARS

2 KINGS 20:5

There is a lot of weeping in the Bible. Hagar cries because she is treated with jealous spite (Gen. 21:16). The people of Israel cry out to God as they suffer cruel injustice in a foreign land (Exod. 3:7). Naomi and her daughters-in-law cry as they look at an uncertain, empty future (Ruth 1:9). Hannah cries because she is barren; she desperately wants children (1 Sam. 1:10). David weeps beneath the weight of his sin (2 Sam. 12:22-23). Hezekiah weeps as he faces up to the reality of his own death (2 Kings 20:5). Peter weeps because he understands that Jesus was right: he has denied his Lord (Luke 22:62). Mary weeps at the tomb, because her Lord has died, and the body is missing (John 20:11).

The soul-racking, utterly desperate, bitter weeping that consumes and exhausts happens time after time in the Bible.

We live in a desperately sad, desperately broken world. Jesus Himself wept in the face of the brutal reality of death.

And as this weeping happens it feels like the end of the story, it feels like all that remains is tears.

Yet, in these instances, the Lord says, 'I have seen your tears.'

The Lord sees, and He tells us He sees because He cares. And having seen, He acts.

The Lord...

... heard the voice of Ishmael crying and promised to make him a great nation.

... used Moses to deliver Israel from Egypt.

... provided Naomi and Ruth with Boaz, a future and a Redeemer.

... remembered Hannah and she later conceived a child.

... forgave David and gave him Solomon.

... comforted Hezekiah and gave him 15 more years.

... restored Peter and made him the rock on which the church was built.

... raised Jesus from the dead and made Mary the first witness to it.

When we weep, there is not always immediate relief. But throughout Scripture we are reminded, as we cry, that the Lord sees, the Lord cares, and the Lord acts for good. However bitter our tears may be, they are not the end of the story.

Loving Father, thank You that You see the pain and anguish no one else sees. Thank You that countless believers before me have cried, and each time You have worked so that their weeping is not the end of the story. Please give me faith that although there is

weeping now, joy will come in the morning, far beyond anything I could have asked or even imagined. Amen.

O Joy that seekest me through pain,
I cannot close my heart to Thee,
I trace the rainbow through the rain,
And see the promise is not vain:
That morn shall tearless be.
George Matheson (1842–1906)

HIS STEADFAST LOVE
ENDURES FOREVER

1 Chronicles 16:34 (ESV)

When our hearts are weary, how we need help to grasp the surprising steadfastness of His enduring love! It can seem so far off, so weak, so waning.

David's declaration here is one of joy, one of delight, and one of surprise. Yes, the Lord's love is unshakably steadfast, but I am not owed this love: it is a love that is baffling and humbling and explosive and glorious – and almost ineffable. However, the Bible writers do give it a go:

- His love is stronger than death and many waters will not quench it (Song. 8:6-7).
- His love will outlast the mountains; it reaches higher than the heavens are above the earth (Isa. 54:10).
- His steadfast love has been lavished on us in Christ (1 John 3:1).
- His love was ours even when we were His enemies (Rom. 5:8).
- His love makes us more than conquerors (Rom. 8:37).

- His steadfast love bends down and cleans the feet of faithless friends (John 13).
- His love cries out for forgiveness of enemies (Luke 23:34).
- His love humbles itself to death – even death on a cross (Phil. 2:8).
- His love endures even though we sin; His love forgives anyone who confesses (1 John 1:8-10).
- His love never fails: neither life nor death nor angels nor demons nor depression nor heartbreak nor war nor persecution nor anything else in all creation can separate us from it (Rom. 8:38).
- His love will not let us go! And it will work for our good in all things (Rom. 8:28).

Oh for hearts to believe it! But how glorious, and reassuring, that long before we have grasped it, His steadfast love for us endures.

Faithful God, thank You so much for the wealth of words that the Bible uses to describe Your love for us. May Your Spirit bear witness to our spirits of the reality of this love; give us eyes to see it, and to see You, the lover of our souls.

O the deep, deep love of Jesus!
Pure, unmeasured, boundless, free,
Rolling as a mighty ocean,
In its fullness over me.
Underneath me, all around me
Is the current of Thy love;
Leading onward, leading homeward,
To Thy glorious rest above.
Samuel Trevor Francis (1834–1925)

I KNOW... MY REDEEMER LIVES

JOB 19:25

I remember once, during a tough few months, reading Job and being struck by these verses:

> God gives me up to the ungodly and casts me into the hands of the wicked... he broke me apart; he seized me by the neck and dashed me to pieces; he set me up as his target (Job 16:11-12 ESV).

Surprisingly, these verses comforted me. I'd often felt like this in the previous years: that God was opposing me, destroying my plans and my peace, and taking away the things I longed for. I was relieved that someone had so boldly articulated such feelings before me.

It also struck me that Job only *thought* God was against him. Actually, God was delighted with him; that's why Satan wanted to attack. I realized that just because it feels like God is opposing me, it doesn't mean He is.

However, Job had suffered in innocence, and I couldn't possibly make that claim for myself! Often the things I have suffered are a murky mess of circumstances and sinfulness. How could I be sure God was not against me?

Because hundreds of years later Jesus felt *exactly* how Job felt. In the Garden of Gethsemane, Jesus wrestled in anguish as He faced what was to come. He pleaded for another way, one in which He would not be handed over to evil men, broken apart and dashed to pieces. He shed tears as He anticipated having God's entire wrath at sin channelled against Him.

Yet, He was willing. He gave Himself up to become the means by which God's justice might be satisfied.

So, how could I be sure God was not against me? Because on the cross, Jesus was opposed by God in my place. The innocent was rejected, so that the guilty might be welcomed.

Gloriously, Jesus' innocence was vindicated in His being raised from the dead. That's why the words of Job are so precious: I know my Redeemer lives!

It may feel like I am God's target, but my living Redeemer is testament to the mind-blowing truth that whatever it may feel like, God is on my side! Jesus suffered for my sin, so when I suffer I can be confident that it is not as a target of God's wrath.

O God, my Rock and my Redeemer, thank You that Your righteous wrath at my sin has been fully satisfied in Jesus. Please help me, when I am tempted to believe that You are against me, to trust in my Redeemer, who bears the marks of Your justice on His hands and sides. Thank You for Your forgiveness; help me to trust in Your willingness to give it to me. For Jesus' sake, Amen.

Lo, Jesus meets us, risen from the tomb;
Lovingly He greets us, scatters fear and gloom;
Let the church with gladness, hymns of triumph sing,
For her Lord now liveth, death hath lost its sting.
Edmond Budry (1854–1932)

THE LORD IS MY SHEPHERD

PSALM 23:1

And I am a sheep.

By which I mean that I am weak, vulnerable and foolish. These things together make a terrible combination, and can make hard times feel complicated: am I suffering because of my weakness? My bad choices? Someone else's bad choices? Because the world in general is terribly broken?

Thankfully, God refers to us as sheep and acknowledges our need for a shepherd. He knows that we are complex and that some of our problems come from our defencelessness against wolves, some from our bad choices to wander off sheer cliff faces, and some from our circumstances (we were born with a certain disposition or a certain lack of wool). Without taking the metaphor any further, the point stands: we are like sheep, a mixture of being weak, vulnerable and foolish.

But the Lord is my shepherd. And this is wonderful news, because He does not respond to my sheepishness, with anger or with disappointment, but by meeting my needs. By being the Good Shepherd.

Across the Scriptures[1] we are assured:

- I am selfish; He lays down His life for mine. I am confused; He knows me thoroughly.
- I am exposed; He brings me into His fold. I am fearful; He speaks comfort.
- I am wayward; He pursues me until He has brought me home. I fear repentance; He rejoices to find me.
- I can't make my own way back; He carries me home and rejoices on the journey.
- I am weary; He gathers me in His arms.
- I am uncertain; He leads me in paths of righteousness.
- I am surrounded by enemies; He makes me a feast in their presence.
- I let Him down; He restores me.
- In my weakness He is strong; in my vulnerability He is tender.
- In my foolishness He is wise; in my helplessness He is my refuge.

We are a strange mixture of weakness and uncertainty and sinfulness, and it can be exhausting trying to parse it all out. But the Lord is sufficient for all our nuances: our psychology, our circumstances, our character flaws and our natural frailty. He delights to gather the whole bundle of our sheepishness in His arms, and carry us close to His heart (Isa. 40:11).

---

1   Based on: Psalm 23, Psalm 100, Isaiah 40, Luke 15, John 10, and Colossians.

The LORD is my shepherd, I have everything I need (Ps. 23:1).

Jesus, my Shepherd, thank You that Your goodness and mercy will be with me every day of my life, and on into eternity. Help me to believe it, amid fear and uncertainty and weakness. Let me know Your goodness as the Shepherd who has laid down His life for me, and may I know Your voice. For Your sake, Amen.

> *I was lost, but Jesus found me,*
> *Found the sheep that went astray,*
> *Threw His loving arms around me,*
> *Drew me back into His way.*
>
> *Days of darkness still come o'er me,*
> *Sorrow's path I often tread,*
> *But His presence still is with me;*
> *By His guiding hand I'm led.*
> F. H. Rowley (1854–1952)

JOY COMES WITH THE MORNING

PSALM 30:5 (ESV)

When I'm suffering a bout of 'low', I do not think that joy will come in the morning.

Instead, I postpone going to bed in a vain attempt to avoid the morning, because in these seasons waking up means more sadness, and more disappointment. Perhaps you've had a chirpy friend say, 'It'll all feel better in the morning,' and you know full well that it will not. In the morning, there will be dread and weariness and probably not enough milk in the fridge for breakfast.

Thankfully, David is not that friend. He doesn't say, 'Joy comes with the morning' from a happy-go-lucky place of unfounded optimism. David wrote Psalm 30 having experienced plenty of weeping. He had known betrayal, false accusation, fearfulness and isolation, and in this psalm he writes of mourning, sackcloth, grief and despair. He has experienced the darkness of night.

The beauty of this verse, like so many others in the Bible, is that it acknowledges the reality of weeping. Life in this world will involve tears and pits and foes. But the testimony of David and the promise of the Bible is that joy will come. And it's not just a vague 'this too shall pass' approach; for David, the joy to come is personal:

> *You have turned for me my mourning into dancing; you have loosed my sackcloth and clothed me with gladness [...] O LORD my God, I will give thanks to you forever!* (Ps. 30:11-12 ESV)

The Lord Himself will bring David joy, the Lord Himself will work to turn it around. And He did: David wasn't in a pit forever. He ended up on a throne! That's the narrative of redemption that begins in Eden and ends in the New Jerusalem: the Lord Himself turns the night's mourning into the morning's dancing. The Lord Himself takes us from the mire to places of majesty!

But how can we be so sure?

Years later, a woman spent a night weeping. She had watched her son die a criminal's death in brutal humiliation. She had stored up a lifetime of memories but her heart had been pierced as she stood by the cross. Her weeping lasted all night, but in the morning, Joy called her name.

Because of that resurrection morning, today we can know with certainty that Jesus is alive. We can know, because He is alive, that the Lord has worked to turn our sadness into delight. And we can know, because He will *always* be alive, that one day the sun will rise and darkness will be swallowed up forever. Easter Sunday morning is the cornerstone of hope in all our weeping nights. Joy will come.

I do not know when I go to sleep tonight whether there will be joy tomorrow morning. Maybe it won't 'all feel better'. But I know Jesus, who weathered the darkest night and then triumphed over it. He wore our sackcloth so we could wear His royal robe. And on that Easter morning, He left the tomb. He is the Morning Star; He is coming soon. Ultimately, joy *will* come in the morning.

Father, hope of the nations, thank You that You are making all things new through Your Son, the Lord Jesus. One day the dawning of Your Light will forever swallow up sadness, sickness and sin. In my dark nights, give me hope that the morning will come. In Jesus' Name, Amen.

See what a morning, gloriously bright
With the dawning of hope in Jerusalem;
Folded the grave-clothes
Tomb filled with light,
As the angels announce Christ is risen!
Stuart Townend and Keith Getty, 2003

HE REMEMBERS... WE ARE DUST

PSALM 103:14

Often, I do not remember that I am dust.

I tend to think that I am more like steel: hard, strong, self-sufficient. When I come to a point when I realize that I am utterly dependent on God, I think that something has gone wrong. I assume that I shouldn't be weak, exhausted or emotionally spent. But needing God is not a result of the Fall. God's plan was always for me to be dependent on Him. I'm not meant to get through my days in self-sufficiency, checking in with the Lord for a bonus boost every now and then.

No.

The Bible confronts this kind of independent self-reliance and challenges those who lean on it: 'Cursed is the man who... makes flesh his strength...' (Jer. 17:5 ESV). The Bible says that if you are getting your strength from yourself, you are turning away from the Lord and in doing so seriously perverting the way things should be.

Instead, there's a better way. Psalm 103 is a rich song of praise to an active, interactive and generous God. He is a God who heals and forgives and redeems, who works righteousness and justice, who shows compassion. This is not a God who made us for independent, self-sufficient living, but instead for a life of dependence on Him!

This is made all the more clear in the life of Jesus. Before He has even begun His ministry He has said that man doesn't live primarily from eating bread but from depending on God – the God who made humanity from dust. Throughout His life, Jesus got tired, overwhelmed, emotional, hungry, and burdened, but He did not sin. In all this His heart did not turn inwards to Himself, but upwards to God, and therefore to blessing. Jesus honoured His Father through total dependence on Him, by the Spirit.

The fact that I cannot survive without God is not a cause for shame. It's okay to be weak, emotional and tired. It's okay to cry out, 'I cannot do today without You!' God never intended me to do today without Him. He never intended any of us to get through any of our days without Him. The Lord delights in those who know their need and trust in His unfailing strength. He is a Father who wants to be involved: He wants to renew us and satisfy us and bless us, bless us, bless us.

For, 'blessed is the one who trusts in the LORD, whose confidence is in him' (Jer. 17:7).

He remembers that we are dust. We might forget it. But when we remember, He calls us to rely on Him. And when we do, He is delighted.

Generous Lord, thank You that the gospel is not about what I will give You, but about what You give me. I come to You today needy and weak, but hopeful, because You are a strong Provider, who delights to meet my needs. Help me know the pleasure You feel in my relying on You that I might do so more and more, for Your glory. Amen.

Fatherlike He tends and spares us;
Well our feeble frame He knows.
In His hands He gently bears us,
Rescues us from all our foes.
Praise Him, praise Him!
Praise Him, praise Him!
Widely as His mercy flows!
H. F. Lyte (1793–1847)

HE DOES WHATEVER PLEASES HIM

PSALM 115:3

A t times, these words can hurt.

Life's circumstances can seem ruthless and harsh, and it's not always easy to understand God's sovereignty amidst life in a messy, broken world. The words, 'He does whatever pleases him,' can feel harsh and hard. They can lodge heavily in our hearts, or thud in our minds like concrete blocks: if God does what He wants, who am I to complain?

And it's true, He does what He pleases. At the end of Job, God doesn't sit down and tell Job all the ways He has been glorified through His servant's faithfulness. He just says, 'Did you make snow? Do you know when mountain goats give birth? Are you commanding the universe?' And of course, were I to answer these questions, my responses would be like Job's: no, and no, and I'm trying but evidently, no. So I too lay my hand over my mouth (Job 40:4).

But the context of these words in Psalm 115 does not suggest harshness, but tenderness.

The words are given in answer to a question. When asked, 'Hasn't your God abandoned you?' the psalmist answers, 'No; he does all he pleases.' God is sovereign, but that does not mean He is far off and callous and aloof and harsh and entitled to do what He wants, so suck it up. No. God is doing what He pleases – which is loving His people.

Our God is the Lord: 'The LORD, the LORD, a God merciful and gracious, slow to anger, and abounding in steadfast love and faithfulness' (Exod. 34:6).

And of course who He is makes an enormous difference to what He wants.

The rest of the psalm shows us this. The Lord does all He pleases, therefore 'he is our help and shield'. The Lord does all He pleases, therefore 'he has remembered us'. The Lord does all He pleases, therefore 'he will bless us, he will bless us, he will bless us'. Again, God wants to help us and shield us and remember us and bless us and love us and be faithful to us. And, hallelujah, God does what He wants!

John Piper writes, 'Our salvation through the death of Christ for us hangs on this: our God is in heaven; he does whatever he pleases.'[1]

---

1   John Piper, 'He Does All That He Pleases', *Desiring God*, 1st September 2012. https://www.desiringgod.org/articles/he-does-all-that-he-pleases (last accessed December 2020).

So, as we limp along paths that feel harsh and steep, we need to remember that God's doing what He wants is not bad news, but glorious good news. It pleases Him to be faithful.

Lord God, thank You that what pleases You is to be steadfast towards Your people in faithfulness and love. Amid the harsh circumstances of life, give me grace to trust Your sovereignty and hope in Your unfaltering faithfulness.

Great is Thy faithfulness, O God my Father,
There is no shadow of turning with Thee!
Thou changest not! Thy compassions they fail not!
As Thou has been, Thou forever will be!
T. O. Chisholm (1886–1960)

THE LORD SETS PRISONERS FREE

PSALM 146:7

I have Psalm 146 written out in full and stuck on my bedroom wall.

I have it there because verse three has been my cling-to verse throughout years of singleness. 'Do not put your trust in princes, in mortal men, who cannot save.'

The psalm draws a striking contrast between men and the Lord. On the one hand there is man – who cannot save, who dies, and whose plans ultimately come to nothing. On the other hand there is the Lord – who made and sustains everything, who remains faithful forever, who upholds the cause of the oppressed, who feeds the hungry, who sets prisoners free, who gives sight to the blind, who lifts up those who are bowed down, who loves and watches and sustains, and whose plans triumph.

No contest: blessed is the one whose help and hope is the God of Jacob! It is He who sets prisoners free.

My bedroom wall psalm has been a joyful reminder to me over the years when I've needed God to calm a hopeful heart, comfort a disappointed heart, or bind up a broken heart. Psalm 146 says that married or not, it is the Lord, rather than any man, who is my help and hope.

I also have it there to remind me about the bigger picture. Take a step back, and my life narrative is not about my love life.

My life story is that I was once a prisoner to sin, fear and death, but then the Lord set me free. I was on death-row, but the King of Heaven died in my place. I was acquitted, liberated, justified and welcomed warmly as His child! And, ever since, the Lord continues to set me free from sin, from fear, from death. Ever since, God's Spirit has testified to my heart: you are no longer a slave! In Christ, you are a son, you are an heir and you are free indeed.

But there is an even bigger picture than that. Take another step back and, hallelujah, the narrative of the world is not about me.

It is about the Lord of heaven. It is about a God who sets captives free.

So, blessed are the widows, the oppressed and the refugees, the slaves in the most horrific circumstances, the prisoners of war and the addicts. Blessed is every fast-bound spirit whose dungeon heart is yet to be flamed with the light of the gospel. Blessed are any whose hope is in the Lord, the God of Israel, because He is infinitely powerful, He is always at work and He alone sets prisoners free.

Gracious Father, God of Jacob. Thank You so much for the countless ways You are at work in the world to do good – to set prisoners free, to provide for widows, to bind up broken hearts. Thank You that all those who have You as their Lord are blessed. Help me believe and see that blessing today, as I trust in You. For Your glory, Amen.

Jesus, the prisoner's fetters breaks,
And bruises Satan's head,
Power unto strengthless souls He speaks,
And life unto the dead!
Charles Wesley (1707–1788)

THE LORD IS MY PORTION

LAMENTATIONS 3:24

Sometimes, when I think about the future, I find the past has long arms. With all its regrets and disappointments, the past reaches through to the present and into the future, and threatens to tear up hope.

The writer of Lamentations must have known this threat. The book is a collection of poems written in the devastation of exile, and the poet wrestles with the anguish of seeing Jerusalem destroyed. The temple has been defiled and all that was precious within it has been taken away. People are starving or slaughtered. The streets are bloodied and desolate. A place that was meant to be a symbol of eternal glory is now in ruins. There's nothing in the writer's current circumstances to offer him hope. There is every reason for the arms of the past to reach forward and tear it to pieces entirely: the past cries 'Loss! Emptiness! Ruin!'

It is remarkable then that these famous verses come in the middle of this anthology of anguish:

Yet this I call to mind, and therefore I have hope: Because of the Lord's great love we are not consumed, for his compassions never fail. They are new every morning; great is your faithfulness (Lam. 3:21-23).

Somehow, right in the middle of the mess, the writer declares: I have hope.

But how?! How can he possibly still have hope? Enter today's five words, 'The Lord is my portion.' And the writer goes on, 'therefore I will hope in him'.

Knowing God is his reason for hope. In the valley of trouble, and ashes, the Lord Himself will be his portion. And whatever our current circumstances, we, like him, can look to the future and ask God to help us forget what is behind… all those disappointments and regrets and failures that reach forward and try to rip up hope. We can ask that He'll keep hope alive. How?

By being our portion!

The brokenness of this world won't be fixed before the new creation. But one day, the poet of Lamentations would see a heavenly Jerusalem that would blow away his expectations for redemption and glory. Its radiance would be 'like a most rare jewel, like a jasper, clear as crystal' (Rev. 21:11 ESV). But in his lifetime, Jerusalem remained in ashes.

Gracious Father, thank You so much that whatever my future may hold, it will also hold Jesus. Thank You that sin and the devil and death could not tear Him up; so, as You are my portion, help me to always carry on in hope! Amen.

Riches I heed not, nor vain, empty praise;
Thou mine inheritance, now and always;
Thou and Thou only first in my heart,
High King of heaven, my treasure Thou art.
Mary Elizabeth Byrne (1881–1931)

I WILL BE WITH YOU

ISAIAH 43:2

God makes this promise to people who are passing through waters and fires to the extent that being drowned or consumed seems a real possibility. He says, 'When you pass through waters, when you walk through fire... I will be with you.'

When God says, 'I will be with you', it's not Him just saying, 'By the way, I'm omnipresent'.

It's not (just) a theological statement; it's a personal assurance. It's a promise for the turbulent times when we might be most tempted to believe it's not true. It's a promise for when it feels like we're drowning, or like our world is on fire. There, God says:

I will be near you.

I will be available to you. I will be your ally.

I will be your friend.

I will be your help, your refuge and your shelter.

Across the globe, as I write, there are believers who are awaiting trials for crimes they have not committed, there are families who, having turned to Christ, have stones thrown at them as they walk home from work; there are believers who are refugees, without earthly belongings, without security, without a clear future and there are believers whose familiar churches are now occupied by ISIS, who witness executions weekly.[1]

To these believers, in these fires, these waters, the LORD says, 'I will be with you.'

Not just 'in theory', but by His Spirit.

For believers who are surrounded by enemies who say, 'You are alone, you are forsaken, you are wretched' – in that moment, when circumstances seem to corroborate these accusations – *then*, the LORD says, 'I will be with you.'

There may be many waters. There may be fiery trials. But no breakers can wash away His steadfast love; no furnace can consume it.

One day, this love unquenchable will bring us safely through death, the most over-whelming of waters, the most intense of fires. But then, like before, but also like never before: 'I will be with you.'

---

1   Examples taken from www.opendoorsuk.org (accessed October 2020).

Immanuel, thank You that even when it most feels like You are not, You are with me. Help me to live the kind of bold, joyful life that makes sense, given the graciousness of this promise. Please comfort those in Your church who have most reason in their circumstances to doubt this promise, and reassure their spirits by Your Spirit. For Jesus' sake, Amen.

Fear not, He is with Thee, O be not dismayed,
For He is thy God and will still give thee aid,
He'll strengthen thee, help thee, and cause thee to stand,
Upheld by His righteous, omnipotent hand.
John Rippon (1751–1836)

HE TOOK UP OUR PAIN

Isaiah 53:4

When I first became a Christian, aged 15, I remember feeling flooded with delight in a science lesson. This was one of two memories I have from science lessons. The other one involved the class discussion of terminal velocity based on what would happen if my teacher threw me, specifically me, out of a helicopter. As you can imagine, delight during science lessons was not normal.

My propensity for not thinking about physics in physics lessons was probably one of the reasons why my teacher framed me as the object of that particular theoretical airborne endeavour. On this day, in this science lesson, as my mind wandered I remembered that my sins were forgiven. Forgiven! The way to my Father had been opened; He was on my side. I remember being amazed: knowing Jesus really makes a difference! Deep joy, even in period 5 physics!

GCSE science has not been my life's greatest hardship. I have had other burdens to carry: depression, loneliness, failure, heartbreak. But what I love about these five words is their reminder that my greatest burden is my sin. Whether I acknowledge it or not, it is my heaviest load, my greatest cause for despair, a weight around my neck that would pull me straight to the bottom of the ocean depths.

But Christ carried my burden to Calvary. He took up my sin and bore the full weight of its penalty in my place. Once and for all, He took up my pain.

This brings comfort because it is a reminder that, whatever else is happening, whatever suffering the past or the present holds, or the future may hold, I've still got at least one Rock-solid reason for joy: my sins are forgiven. Today, I may have to face many trials, but I do not have to face them carrying the burden of my sin. He took up my pain; He bore my sorrows. My sin is as far away from me as the east is from the west. On days of pain, my sins are no longer mine to carry!

And the cross is a beautiful reminder that Jesus knows how to take up pain.

When my burdens seem too large, I can cast them on Jesus and trust that He will take them up. He has made my burdens His business; with His almighty arm He has hurled my iniquities into the depths of the sea (Micah 7:19). In His strength and grace and kindness and service, Jesus took up my ultimate burden and carried it to the cross; of course He can also carry the other, smaller burdens that may be mine today.

He took up my pain, and He takes it up still.

God, my strength and my salvation, thank You that You have dealt, once and for all, with my greatest problem. Thank You that Your Son carried my burden to the cross, and made the pain that should have been mine His own. As I learn to love these truths, make me more and more willing to trust my other burdens to Him too. For His glory, Amen.

Though Satan should buffet, though trials should come,
Let this blessed assurance control:
That Christ has regarded my helpless estate,
And has shed His own blood for my soul!
Horatio G. Spafford (1828–1888)

I CAME TO CALL SINNERS

MARK 2:17 (ESV)

The Pharisees grumbled to the disciples of Jesus, 'Why does he eat with sinners?'

And when Jesus heard it, He said to them, 'It is not the healthy who need a doctor, but the sick. I have not come to call the righteous, but sinners.'

And in doing so, Jesus declared with decisive and irrevocable glory: I am the friend of sinners.

Every time I remember this I am relieved. If Jesus is the friend of sinners, then I qualify. Hallelujah! He didn't come to call good people, but sinners. What 'qualifies' me for Him is my need for Him.

There are thousands of ways in which my 'inner Pharisee' would tell me that I'm not worthy of Jesus; that Jesus wants happy, free, confident, fearless, fully sanctified followers.

So when I approach Jesus, I know the grumbling will start.

The inner Pharisees will say, 'Why would Jesus eat with those who are sad; who wander off like sheep? Why would

Jesus have anything to do with you – you're insecure, you're foolish, and you don't even know how to pray!?'

But to the inner Pharisees, Jesus speaks:

It is not the carefree that need a Comforter, but the mourning. It is not the free that need a Liberator, but the enslaved.

- It is not the sun-soaked who need a Light, but those who dwell in darkness.
- It is not those whose futures are all mapped out who need a Hope, but the despairing.
- It is not the confident who need a Refuge, but the insecure.
- It is not the intelligent who need the Wisdom of God, but the foolish.
- It is not those with functional relationships who need a Counsellor, but the heartbroken.
- It is not the competent who need a Guide, but the confused.
- It is not the calm who need the Prince of Peace, but those who are stressed.
- It is not the righteous that need the Crucified Christ, but sinners.

Jesus comes to be good news to the worst of situations. He comes to make the saddest hearts sing, to set free those who are most oppressed and most addicted. He brings sight to those who are blind and hope to situations that are inescapably and brutally hopeless; and He shines a light on those who dwell in the most suffocating and impenetrable darkness.

There is no one so poor, so weak, so sinful, so oppressed or so beyond hope that they do not qualify for Him. Hallelujah!

Jesus, friend of sinners. Friend of mine! Thank You that You did not come to be served, but to serve us in our need. We are sinners, we are confused, we are stressed, we are broken, and we need You. Thank You that You came for wretches like us! Amen.

How sweet the name of Jesus sounds,
In the believer's ear!
He soothes our sorrows,
Heals our wounds,
And drives away our fear!
John Newton (1725–1807)

HE RAN AND EMBRACED HIM

LUKE 15:20 (ESV)

These five words tell the story of a homecoming. The image Jesus paints in this description of the Father, pelting his way down a dirty road, is one of an active, abundantly generous, enthusiastic, welcoming, kind God.

As Jesus tells the story of the Rejected One running to embrace and kick-start a party for the Rejecter, the God I have believed in – who is passive and stingy and aloof – must be banished. Jesus knows the Father like no one knows the Father, and He says of Him, 'He ran and embraced him.'

The God and Father of our Lord Jesus Christ is running towards us, bridging the distance between us and Him and inviting us to celebrate our return!

God is the God of homecoming. All three of the Luke 15 'lost and found' narratives end with a party. There is great rejoicing in heaven when a sinner repents. In the same way that the father in the parable sets off to greet the disgraced son – with warmth and joy, with robe and ring in hand, even while the wretched rebel is still far off – there is great rejoicing in heaven when even one sinner comes home!

Oh how could my return merit such a welcome? Because my homecoming is tightly wrapped up in another's. After Jesus died, and was raised, He ascended to heaven. His was the ultimate homecoming. How the angels must have whooped and wondered! How the heavens must have rung! The Champion has conquered! The price is paid! Death is swallowed up in victory! Glory to the Risen, Conquering Son!

But the good news is that Heaven's Champion is my champion too. By the infinite grace of the Father, those who are His share His welcome, His robe, His ring; the delight of the Father in this Son's homecoming is the delight of the Father that we too are no longer lost, but found, made sons, made heirs and destined to be raised up by Christ, and in Christ, at the last day.

When I'm low, it's so good to know that my welcome is tied to Christ's glory. As I'm forgiven and celebrated, Jesus' kindness and power and grace are demonstrated as glorious. Every time there is a party in heaven to celebrate a sinner who comes home, there is a party in heaven to celebrate the One who brought, and bought, them home.

Abba Father, thank You for Heaven's Champion who has entered the Most Holy Place on my behalf and has been welcomed home as Lord of all! Thank You that my being rescued by Jesus gives You great joy; may it give me increasing joy too. Amen.

O perfect redemption, the purchase of blood!
To every believer the promise of God:
The vilest offender who truly believes,
That moment from Jesus a pardon receives!

Praise the Lord, praise the Lord! Let the earth hear his voice.
Praise the Lord, praise the Lord! Let the people rejoice.
O come to the Father through Jesus, the Son,
And give Him the glory, Great things He has done!
Frances van Alstyne (1820–1915)

NEITHER DO I CONDEMN YOU

JOHN 8:11

The woman in John 8 is brought to Jesus having been caught committing adultery. She has been found in the act. The teachers of the law excitedly bring her to Jesus knowing she is worthy of death, absolutely confident of their verdict: she's guilty! And yet Jesus says in verse 7, 'Let any one of you who is without sin be the first to throw a stone...' And when everyone walks away, He says in verse 11, 'Neither do I condemn you.' They all leave, because they know their own guilt. Gradually, one by one, they know they do not have the authority to condemn.

There is only one who does, but He says, 'Neither do I condemn you.'

This story is really good news to me as someone who has a tendency to feel condemned by all manner of things: my singleness, my selfishness, my sarcasm, my self-absorption....

Sometimes the condemnation I feel is justified; sometimes society, or other sinners or sickness speak it falsely.

But this story reminds me that Jesus chases all condemnation away. He speaks words of life over all condemnation that echoes in my mind: whether my feelings of guilt come from my own sin, from society's warped expectations, from depression, or from the Accuser himself, Jesus still says, 'Neither do I condemn you!'

There is now no condemnation for those in Christ Jesus. Even in the ways where I am most like this woman – where my sin is most obvious and my guilt most indisputable, Jesus will not condemn. He who died for my sins and was raised for our justification has taken His place on the throne. From His position as the Name above all Names He declares: Neither do I condemn you.

God of mercy, what an incredible promise You have made that because of Jesus there is no more condemnation for me to face. Help me to believe it as I live surrounded by voices – from without and within – that would condemn me. Let me hear the gracious voice of Jesus saying, 'Neither do I condemn you; go and sin no more.' Amen.

Other refuge have I none, hangs my helpless soul on Thee,
Leave, ah leave me not alone, still support and comfort me:
All my trust on Thee is stayed, all my help from Thee I bring:
Cover my defenceless head, with the shadow of Thy wing!
Charles Wesley (1707–1788)

IT IS GOD WHO JUSTIFIES

ROMANS 8:33

I t is God who justifies.

This is Paul's five-word answer to the question, 'Who will bring any charge against those whom God has chosen?'

The answer is not a promise that no one will bring any charges. Across the world countless believers face actual court cases where they stand accused of blasphemy or apostasy, or of betraying their national identity, their communities or their families.

Daily, believers face all kinds of accusations – of arrogance, of intolerance, of selfishness, many of which are right. Facing charges and condemnation was part and parcel of life for the Christians Paul was writing to. That's why he asks the question!

The key to the answer is the emphasis: GOD is the one who justifies.

The one who not only forgives us, but who also declares us righteous cannot be trumped. There is no higher authority. And there is no other means.

If I am striving for it in my quiet-time record, my strength of character, my CV or through sorting out my appearance, the efforts will be futile.

There is only one who can justify, and it is not me.

In all my dieting, self-discipline and determination for success, I need to remember; none of those things can secure me the verdict I need. It is God who justifies.

And He has.

Thank You, Lord of all, that it is not me who justifies: it is not my holiness, my character, my discipline, my achievements that put me right with You. As if they could! Thank You that it is You, the God of heaven, who justifies. Only Your verdict matters, and You've given me Your declaration of 'RIGHTEOUS!' In Jesus' name. Thank You. Amen.

Behold Him there, the Risen Lamb-
The perfect spotless righteousness!
The great unchangeable I am!
The King of glory and of grace!
One with Himself I cannot die,
My soul is purchased with His blood.
My life is hid with Christ on high,
With Christ my Saviour and my God!
Charitie Lees Bancroft (1841–1923)

HE IS INTERCEDING FOR US

ROMANS 8:34 (BSB)

Times of trial – whether they come from external affliction or internal distress – often make me wrestle with a truth that is often taken for granted: God loves me. But how could He, I think? When life feels like a series of unrelenting tribulations, how can I possibly trust that the Sovereign Lord is on my side?

In Romans 8, Paul recognizes that circumstances may give us cause to doubt God's commitment to us. He acknowledges suffering and distress and persecution as factors that might have us believe we have been separated from Jesus' love.

He acknowledges the devastating circumstances the Christians he is writing to face: they 'are being killed all the day long… regarded as sheep to be slaughtered' (Rom. 8:36). Life is lived in the shadow of death: they endure public shame, they are considered worthless, pitiful, as sheep to be slaughtered. But Paul specifically mentions all these circumstances to make it explicitly clear to the believer: even in this, you are not separated from Christ's love. Nothing can separate you.

Through Christ's love, he writes, you are more than conquerors! And love here is no abstract concept: it's a reality, an action, an ongoing conversation between our brother, Jesus, and His Father, on our behalf. Right now, in the seat of highest authority in the entire universe, Jesus is on our side. Right now, He is speaking out for us in love. His love for us is not only something expressed in the past (though it is) – it's also something He is currently in the process of expressing to us as He mentions us in prayer.

Whatever else is going on in our lives, right now, something else is also happening. Christ is at God's right hand, talking to His Father about us. As He has loved us, at the cross, He continues to love us now. From His position at the right hand of the Father, Jesus is loving us and interceding for us, praying perfect prayers in our place – and nothing can separate us from His love.

Lord Jesus, my great High Priest. My prayers are weak and feeble – but Yours are strong and perfect. Thank You that You are praying for me – today, all day. Today You are loving me, as You always have. Whatever I may face, today – trouble or danger or shame – help me to remember Your unfailing love and that You are praying for me at the Father's right hand. Thank You that Your prayers will always be answered, for Your glory, Amen.

Blessed assurance, Jesus is mine:
O what a foretaste of glory divine!
Heir of salvation, purchase of God;
born of His Spirit, washed in His blood.
Fanny J. Crosby (1844–1915)

GOD CHOSE WHAT IS WEAK

1 Corinthians 1:27 (ESV)

After I left university, I went to work for a mission organization in France for two years.

I lived on the Côte d'Azur and it was beautiful (or 'Nice', as everyone who had the chance joked!). But my time there also felt brutal: I wasn't good at French, I had few meaningful relationships, my battle with failure and disappointment seemed unrelenting and unsuccessful, and I became very depressed.

I frequently remembered these words and was bewildered by them: that despite the enormity of my weakness, my sinfulness, my tendency to be fearful, intensely emotional, tired, God said He chose me. Daily, I struggled to believe it.

But at the end of that time, a friend who I had begun to read the Bible with sent me a letter that included these words:

When I think about how much you struggled here, it convinces me much more of your message. No one would do what you did for fun. Thank you for letting me witness your battle and for being human about your struggle. Your honesty has led me to this place of hope.

Her words were deeply moving. They showed me that when God says He chooses what is weak, His view of weakness is more profound than I can imagine. My friend had seen that I was weak in ways I would never have wanted her to: foolish in the world's eyes, foolish in my lack of French, prone to struggle, prone to sinfulness, battling with pain – and yet in it she'd seen Jesus. He took away every reason I had to boast in myself, yet gave me a reason to boast in Him.

This is the way God has always chosen to work. In the same way that God chose the foolishness of a cross to put to shame the wisdom of the wise, He chooses weak, cracked jars of clay and uses them to carry His treasure to the world.

God of the broken, thank You that You delight to put the treasure of Your gospel in weak jars of clay like me, because it shows so clearly that the gospel is about Your power, and grace, and strength – and not mine. Use me today in all my weakness, to bear witness to Your kindness and ability to rescue and redeem and keep me boasting only in You. Amen.

We rest on Thee, our shield and our defender!
We go not forth alone against the foe,
Strong in Thy strength, safe in Thy keeping tender,
We rest on Thee and in Thy name we go!

We go in faith, our own great weakness feeling,
And needing more each day Thy grace to know:
Yet from our hearts a song of triumph peeling –
'We rest on Thee, and in Thy name we go!'
Edith Gilling Cherry (1872–1897)

CHRIST DIED FOR OUR SINS

1 Corinthians 15:3

*C*hrist died for our sins is a truth that cuts through every misconception I have of God as being uncaring; it's His love articulated in one earth-shattering, historical fact. When I am tempted to feel abandoned by God, it's a reminder that Jesus was abandoned by Him so that I would never be. It reminds me that God is not a tyrant; He is not cold, He is not aloof, He is not unmoved by a suffering world.

Christ died for our sins is not something I can believe while simultaneously believing that God is holding something back from me. It calls me back to believe in His abundant generosity; Christ died. God did not withhold His Son, and His Son did not withhold His life; Father and Son willingly gave all They had for my sake. Whatever else is going on in my disappointment, it cannot be that God is stingy; He's already given me Jesus.

Christ died for our sins cuts through the burden of guilt that so often entangles my heart. The thorns and thistles of shame are sliced to pieces by this remarkable gospel: the price has been paid. The blood of the Prince of Glory has been poured out, and my sins have been dealt with.

Christ died for our sins is the crushing of Satan's head. The bite of the heel predicted in Genesis 3 is the beginning of the curse reversed; it starts with my liberation from the mastery of sin – it ends with the redemption of all of creation.

Christ died for our sins is a beautiful anthem for the unity of the church; we were all weak, all worthless, all wandering. But our Good Shepherd went and found each of us, and He laid down His life. Where we were once utterly isolated, we've been brought near – we're in it together, we've been made one.

Christ died for our sins! These five words bear witness to a truth that has revolutionized the entire course of history, a truth that gives us countless reasons to rejoice!

God of the gospel, thank You that when I was weak and lost and sinful, when I was an object of wrath and Your enemy, because You loved me, Christ died for my sins. Help me to believe it more and more, and to praise You more and more as I do. Amen.

And can it be, that I should gain
An interest in the Saviour's love?
Died He for me, who caused His pain,
For me, who Him, to death pursued!
Amazing love! How can it be,
That Hhou, my God, should die, for me!?
Charles Wesley (1707-1788)

WHAT IS UNSEEN IS ETERNAL

2 CORINTHIANS 4:18

When I am feeling at my lowest, I find it hard to imagine that I will ever feel any different. Even though I've suffered cycles of depression and relief for years, when the next low arrives, the sadness feels heavier and more real than anything I've ever experienced; I can't imagine that the darkness will ever lift. Though I know depression skews my perspective, when I'm in it, I feel like I'm seeing things more clearly than ever.

Depression can be like being set in concrete: it's very difficult for your mind to find the energy to stagger beyond the very short cycle of misery you're in right now to contemplate anything in the future at all. Depression tightly wraps up hope in a shroud, and then leaves it to rest somewhere behind an unrelenting wall of stone.

This is why these five words are so profoundly encouraging.

However it may feel, however weighty the suffering is, however convinced I may be that my bleak outlook on the future is accurate and inescapable: what is unseen is eternal.

The pattern of history is that when Hope is wrapped in a shroud and laid to rest in a tomb, it does not stay there forever.

Because Hope was put in a tomb. But three days later, He was out on the beach, eating brunch with His friends. And now He is in heaven: shining like the sun at its strongest, waiting to come again to reign. He may be unseen, for now, but He's eternal.

Despair is wrong. I don't mean this so much as a moral statement as a fact. Despair says: 'Death and sadness and sorrow last forever.' But it's wrong.

Suffering is weighty and bitter and often feels more real than anything else; but it is passing away, it is transient. Suffering is to glory what dust is to a radiant city built of gold.

What is unseen is eternal, so we do not lose heart.

God of all comfort, thank You for the promise that these light and momentary troubles are achieving for me a glory that far outweighs them. Often troubles seem weighty and inescapable, so I thank You that it is what is unseen that will last forever. Keep me hoping in Jesus, who I will see one day, and who is even now more real than anything in all of creation. Help me believe it, for His glory. Amen.

Like the shining sun in its noonday strength,
We now see the glory of Your wondrous face:
Once that face was marred, now You're glorified;
And Your words, like a two-edged sword have mighty power:
'I am he that liveth! That liveth and was dead!
Behold, I am alive forever more!'
Dave Fellingham, 1983

I AM CRUCIFIED WITH CHRIST

GALATIANS 2:20 (KJV)

The big argument of Paul in Galatians is: you are justified by faith in Jesus.

'I am crucified with Christ' is a testament to the fact that our identity was tied up with Christ at the most profound moment of the universe. These words show us that the death of Jesus goes beyond providing forgiveness, and beyond paying our debt – glorious as that is.

The wonder of this verse is that Jesus has paid the penalty for the inadequacy of our own lives and has given us His record, His life, His very self.

This is wonderful news to anyone used to weighing the significance of their own life and finding it wanting. At times in my life I have lived by statements like:

'The life I live, I live striving in the hope that I will achieve something worthwhile.'

'The life I live, I live in fear that I will never be enough.'

'The life I live, I live by desperate self-justification because that's all I've got.'

'The life I live, I live in desperate hope that someone will love me and vindicate my worth.'

'The life I live, I live by banking on my own strength, my own sufficiency, my own righteousness.'

But Paul's argument in Galatians offers a better way to finish that sentence.

He says, 'The life I live, I live by faith in the Son of God, who loved me and gave himself for me.'

My life is not rendered meaningful in my behaviour, or in my reputation, or in my validation, or in my relationships, or in anything else.

My life is rendered meaningful because the Champion of heaven loved me because He lived a perfect life of love; because He took on my sin and crowned me with His righteousness. That's what I am living for. I'm living my life by unshakeable love. I'm living by looking to Jesus – who loved me, and gave Himself for my forgiveness, and for my life's justification.

I am crucified with Christ, and Christ lives in me.

Gracious Father, help me to live my life today trusting in Jesus who has loved me and given Himself for me. May I let go of all those other ways in which I try to find significance, and cling fast to the knowledge that the King of the Universe died so I might live. Help me to live to the praise of His glory, Amen.

He took my sins and my sorrows,
He made them His very own
He bore the burden to Calvary,
He suffered and died alone.

How marvellous! How wonderful!
And my song will ever be
How marvellous! How wonderful!
Is my Saviour's love for me!
Charles H. Gabriel (1856–1932)

WE LIVE BY THE SPIRIT

GALATIANS 5:25

A CONVERSATION WITH GOD

Many mornings I wake up and think about all I have to do
in planning,
in completing life's admin tasks,
in all the complexities of relationships and life, and then I
think about all You call me to be in love and self-sacrifice and
joy
and I bury my head under the covers and say, 'I can't do this.'
On these mornings I lie in bed at the foot of a mountain
mustering the strength to put on climbing boots, and You
hear the conviction with which I say,
'I can't do this.'
And I expect You to say; 'But you must!' But You don't.
Instead You say, 'I know.'
I say, 'I cannot do this.'
And You say, with patience and warmth, 'I know.' You say, in
fact:

'Cursed is the one who depends on flesh for strength', and in my weariness I feel the weight of that truth.

You say, 'Cursed is the one whose help is man, who turns away from the LORD.'

You say, 'You can't do this.' And I say, 'I know.'

But then You say:

'Blessed is the one who trusts in the LORD, whose confidence is in him...'

You say: 'They will be like a tree planted by water, that sends out its roots by the stream. It does not fear when heat comes, its leaves are always green.'

You say, 'I will be your strength.'

You say, 'Keep in step with the Spirit.'

You never intended for me to get out of bed in my own strength; You never called me to seek out a hero within.

You never asked me to get up and give You something from my own tired, tainted flesh.

Each morning Your promises and mercies are new, each morning You call me to get up and receive.

Each morning You offer strength for the day, grace for the hurdles, a hero in the heavens and Your Spirit in my heart. And so I get out of bed, trusting that as promised, You will fill empty hands, You will strengthen weak knees, and You will, by Your Spirit, bring life to my dry bones.

Holy Spirit, I know that I cannot do today in my own strength, and so I turn to You, trusting that You will give me everything I need for today. May I be like a tree planted by streams of living water that never ceases to bear fruit, with roots that go down deep into Your all-sufficient strength, that You might be glorified in my life. Amen.

So Spirit come, put strength in every stride,
Give grace for every hurdle,
That we may run with faith to win the prize,
Of a servant, good and faithful!
As saints of old still line the way,
Retelling triumphs of His grace,
We hear their call, and hunger for the day,
When with Christ we'll stand in glory!
Stuart Townend & Keith Getty, 2009

HE HIMSELF IS OUR PEACE

EPHESIANS 2:14

The world is weighed down with darkness. And how can our hearts not be weighed down too?

So often we are confronted by it in a way that is overwhelming: stories of child abuse, unprecedented terror, devastation of homes and countries. There is so much – personal and political – that is impossible to understand; how we've got here and how we'll ever escape seems beyond our fathoming. Suffering is cumbersome and complex, inscrutable and isolating: it's hard to hope when we can't imagine what a solution to it might look like.

Into this world then, the words of the angel at the birth of Jesus are striking: 'Peace on earth!'

The enormous relief is that they weren't proclaiming the arrival of a neat philosophy or manifesto, a state of soul or a simplistic solution.

Hallelujah, they were not pointing within: to our own minds and spirits – but to a person, a baby, wrapped in cloth, and lying in a manger. As He lay in that manger, Jesus began to plumb the depths of our darkness and our suffering, and as He grew, He began to redeem.

Jesus is a person: a historical, glorious, redeeming, refreshingly complex person. He can meet the complexity of the darkness. He can fathom the nuances of a thousand shadows. And He will not be overcome.

He Himself is our peace.

Isaiah wrote: 'The people walking in darkness have seen a great light' (Isa. 9:2).

The darkness of our sadness, suffering and sin is not simple, and neither is its solution. But this does not mean He is not adequate for these things. To the contrary, it means He is able to deal with them more comprehensively, more rigorously, and more gloriously then we ever could imagine. He is not just a person, but the ultimate person. He is not just a bringer of peace, He is our Peace. And He has been given to those walking in darkness.

The promise to those walking in darkness is not a neat answer to unpick the confusion or wrap up the pain. The promise to them is Jesus, the Prince of Peace.

Lord Jesus, Prince of Peace – my peace. Help me to consider everything else as a loss compared to the surpassing worth of knowing You. Amid all the struggles and suffering in life, may I know You better, in all Your redeeming power. For Your glory, Amen.

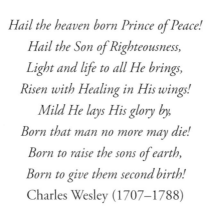

Hail the heaven born Prince of Peace!
Hail the Son of Righteousness,
Light and life to all He brings,
Risen with Healing in His wings!
Mild He lays His glory by,
Born that man no more may die!
Born to raise the sons of earth,
Born to give them second birth!
Charles Wesley (1707–1788)

OUR CITIZENSHIP IS IN HEAVEN

PHILIPPIANS 3:20

I grew up in Rwanda and came back to the UK when I was 12. During my first two years of secondary school, I felt very strange and, if I ever forgot my strangeness, a chorus of fellow pupils were on hand to remind me: 'Oh you're the girl from Sweden!'; 'You're from Canada'; or my all-time favourite, 'You're from Saudi Africa'!

I have often been keenly aware of deep feelings of alienation. But through the years I've come to see that these feelings find their ultimate root in the Garden of Eden: where there could have been security and citizenship, there was exile and exclusion.

Don't I deserve to be excluded? I've turned my back on love; I've destroyed the good gifts in my life; I've been arrogant in the pursuit of independence. I've had the sweet taste of greedily consumed fruit turn bitter in my mouth. I've felt the deep sting of shame. I've hidden from Justice's pure glare.

So how can it be that my citizenship is in heaven?

Because the ultimate citizen of heaven was born, lived and died an outsider.

Heaven's Beloved was born in a manger, misunderstood by His family, betrayed by His friends. The teachers of the Scriptures that bore witness to Him mocked Him. A government whose power came from Him punished Him. He died the most shameful death imaginable, on a cross, outside of the city. He died with even His Father's back turned on Him, with every possible door shut in His face.

Jesus, who had embraced the warm love of heaven that I spurned, was excluded from the presence of God so that I might be welcomed in. In my place, the Beloved marched up to the flaming sword of justice that kept me from citizenship in heaven; it fell on Him so that it would never fall on me.

Because of Jesus, I am no outsider. He's been Heaven's outsider, so I might be welcomed home.

God of the nations, thank You that You have welcomed me in, and have said that I belong to You. Knowing that I am secure, help me live today forgetting myself and serving others. May I do all I can to invite other people into Your fellowship, welcoming them as You have welcomed me. Amen.

You held out Your arms, I see them still
You never left, You never will
Running to embrace me, now I know
Your cords of love will always hold.
Mercy's robe, a ring of grace
Such favor undeserved
You sing over me and celebrate
The rebel now Your child.
Meghan and Ryan Baird, 2009

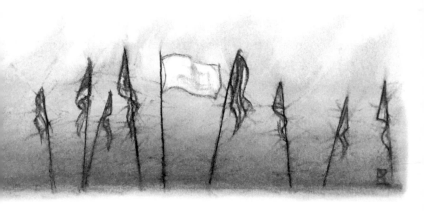

GOD HAS SPOKEN TO US

HEBREWS 1:2

Sometimes when we suffer, the mystery of the pain feels overwhelming. Often when I am most depressed I find myself spiralling as I desperately try to understand the darkness: why on earth doesn't He take away the pain? I cannot fathom a reason why I have the temperament, biology and life circumstances that have led me to a place that feels so completely pointless, so completely broken.

It's tempting in these times to focus on all the unanswered questions and to feel at first perplexed, and then, when an answer doesn't come, to give way to despair. Amid the pain, it is easy to desperately wonder why God is silent.

But God is not silent. God has spoken to us.

So often I judge God by what He hasn't said to me, far more than by what He has. I've created a version of God that's an amalgamation of what the Bible says, and what my circumstances and my heart say. Unsurprisingly, the God created in my own image is not that great!

Deuteronomy 29:29 says: 'The secret things belong to the LORD our God, but the things that are revealed belong to us and to our children...' (ESV).

The revealed things are a gift to us – they're something for us to lean all our weight upon in our darkness and weakness and fragility. The revealed things liberate us to trust God with the things that He keeps secret.

And when God speaks, He makes sense: He has revealed Himself and He's been clear. He is not a puzzle that the cleverest people solve, or a reward that the godliest people earn: no! He has spoken to us by His Son. In Jesus, He has made Himself known.

Through Jesus, God has said, 'I am with you', 'I forgive you', 'I am for you' and so much more.

Although there are some things God has not said, He has not left us in total darkness. He gives us what we need: the words, the Word – to comfort us, to strengthen us, to bring us life.

Almighty God, it seems as though there are many areas of my life where I have cried out to You, and You have been silent. But I am so grateful for how You have spoken to me by Your Son. Give me grace to lean heavily on what You have said, and to build my life on those foundations. May what You have revealed give me peace about those things that remain a mystery. Amen.

I cannot tell how silently He suffered,
As with His peace He graced this place of tears,
Or how His heart upon the Cross was broken,
The crown of pain to three and thirty years.
But this I know, He heals the broken-hearted,
And stays our sin, and calms our lurking fear,
And lifts the burden from the heavy laden,
For yet the Saviour, Saviour of the world, is here.
William Young Fullerton (1857–1932)

AND HE UPHOLDS THE UNIVERSE

HEBREWS 1:3 (ESV)

The reason this 'Bible Bit' starts with 'and' is not because I was trying to get up to the word count but because I deliberately wanted to connect these five words with the previous five, and then with all of the other five-word packages.

God has spoken to us by His Son and He upholds the universe.

Christ died for our sins and He upholds the universe.

He Himself is our peace and He upholds the universe.

These five words are a timely reminder: God has power to do what He has promised.

In times where I've felt most battered by life, I have deeply needed this assurance.

The God who has said that He will be with me, that He has forgiven me, that He has seen my tears, that He is at work in all things for my good – this God, revealed fully in Jesus – He upholds the universe.

I should feel a little incredulous as I ponder these words.

The biblical writers did not take for granted the fact that the Lord, who made the starry host, interacted with little humans. They wondered at it! They looked at the ineffable magnitude of the heavens and were brought to their knees in awe; the universe-upholding Maker had made Himself known, and with tenderness and care!

> *When I consider your heavens, the work of your fingers,*
> *the moon and the stars, which you have set in place,*
> *what is man that you are mindful of him,*
> *and the son of man that you care for him?*
> (Ps. 8:3-4 ESV).

As I face trials and tribulations and am overwhelmed with my own foolish, flailing powerlessness, four of these five words remind me of God's power to help me, for He upholds the universe, and the other word, 'and', reminds me of His great, gracious promise. He who keeps planets in motion, who keeps countless hearts beating, mighty tides turning, and mountain ranges from tumbling into oceans, has spoken to us in His Son.

What wonder, Lord of the Universe, that You would care for me – that You would speak to me. Give me faith in Your power, and humility as I depend on You, knowing that the whole of Creation is sustained by Your power, through Jesus Christ our Lord. Amen.

Crown Him with many crowns, the Potentate of time!
Creator of the rolling spheres, ineffably sublime!
All hail, Redeemer, hail, for Thou hast died for me;
Thy praise shall never, ever fail, through all eternity!
Matthew Bridges (1800–1894) & Godfrey Thring
(1823–1903)

YOU HAVE COME TO... JESUS!

HEBREWS 12:22-24

Today's earth-shattering words are the crowning evidence of God's love to us in the gospel. They are a five-word reminder that the gospel is not about God getting us into heaven, but about God giving Jesus to us for our everlasting joy. These verses from Hebrews work to a glorious climax of everything that is ours in the gospel:

> *You have come to Mount Zion and to the city of the living God, the heavenly Jerusalem, and to innumerable angels in festal gathering, and to the assembly of the firstborn who are enrolled in heaven, and to God, the judge of all, and to the spirits of the righteous made perfect, and to Jesus, the mediator of a new covenant, and to the sprinkled blood that speaks a better word than the blood of Abel* (Heb. 12:22-24 ESV).

Yes, in Jesus we become citizens of the heavenly Jerusalem. Yes, we get an invite to a party of angels. Yes, our names are written in heaven. But more than that - we come to God!

Abel's blood cried out for his brother's condemnation. But Jesus' blood cries out for His brothers' justification. And justification is not an end in itself: it's the means by which we can come to the Father. Jesus' blood cries, 'Come to the Father! Come to me!'

The ultimate gift of the gospel isn't the city or the party, as glorious as they will be. The ultimate gift of the gospel is God Himself! His universe-creating, mercy-showering, eternally-loving self!

Not only does God say, 'You belong to me', but in His staggering generosity He says, 'and I belong to you'.

So whatever else may come to us in life – be it sickness, or loneliness, or unemployment, or poverty, or war – wherever else the road may lead, the Lord has also said, you have come to Me! Whatever other blessings you may get in the gospel, you also get Jesus, and you also get Me. I am your portion, I am your destiny and I am your everlasting joy: you have come to Me!

God Most High, thank You that I am Yours, and You are mine. Thank You that You are my portion, my destiny, my refuge and my joy. You are the Greatest Treasure reality affords and because of Your mercy, I can know You forever. Give me joy in these truths that no other life-portion can take away, that You might be glorified. Amen.

No condemnation now I dread,
Jesus, and all in Him is mine!
Alive in Him, my living head,
And clothed in righteousness divine!
Bold I approach the eternal throne,
And claim the crown, through Christ, my own!
Charles Wesley (1707–1788)

NOW YOU HAVE RECEIVED MERCY

1 PETER 2:10

I recently read an article that was entitled: '33 Key Signs You're Not Living The Life You Deserve'. The presupposition behind much of its advice was that the life you deserve is better than the life you currently have: if you don't enjoy the life you currently have, you must deserve better.

The Bible says something very different. It says something uncomfortable, exposing, and brutal, but something that is fundamentally better news. The Bible says that those who are self-obsessed, self-serving and self-congratulating have only earned themselves death. Those who are twisted in on themselves, who have cursing, death-ridden tongues, who take the road of destruction, who have lived without any fear of God, have earned death. The Bible says: all have sinned, all have fallen short and all are worthy of death. The Bible says that the life I deserve is not the life I want! The life I deserve, it says, is death.

What I need is something that is far better news than 'the life I deserve'. What I need is mercy. In *The Merchant of Venice* Shakespeare said that mercy is 'mightiest in the mightiest.' There is therefore the mightiest of hope in the words of Psalm 103, verse 10: '[The LORD] does not treat us as our sins deserve.' What wonder, that the Mightiest might exercise such mercy!

The Bible says: you deserve judgment, but you can receive mercy instead.

What a relief! Countless times in my life I have looked to the future filled with dread, aware of the grimness within and what it has earned me. But these five words cut through it: now you have received mercy. Countless times in my life I have looked at the present filled with bitterness, convinced that my pale collection of reluctant good deeds put God in my debt. But these five words cut through it: now you have received mercy.

As I look to the future, process my past and experience the present, sinful though I may be, there is bright hope ahead, because now, because of Jesus, I have received mercy.

Merciful God, strength for today and bright hope for tomorrow are blessings all mine, with ten thousand beside! Even though what I deserved was condemnation, You took that condemnation Yourself instead. Thank You. Give me a glimpse of the unquenchable hope that is mine, because I have received Your mercy, and, as I enjoy it, would Your mercy overflow to others through me. In Jesus' Name, Amen.

Pardon for sin, and peace that endureth,
Thine own dear presence to cheer and to guide:
Strength for today, and bright hope for tomorrow,
Blessings all mine with ten thousand beside!
T. O. Chisholm (1866–1960)

HE IS FAITHFUL AND JUST

1 JOHN 1:9

Anguished moments in a moonlit garden,

Droplets of blood fall heavy,

Each its own plea for another way.

But because You are faithful, You take the cup:

It storms with Heaven's fury.

But You take it, and start to sip; You will stagger beneath its wine.

Because You are faithful, You leave the Garden, for Golgotha.

You alone deserve to stay in the Garden;

You alone have lived with the love that makes You welcome there.

But because You are faithful, to me,

You take the road to exile, to execution.

You take that road so I can walk by another way.

As You wipe Your tears and see the torches approach,

You strain for a joy set before: the joy of mercy?

More – the joy of justice.

Because You are just, my darkest nights are free from the shadow cast by that cup.

There may be anguished moments, but there is no wrath left for me to drink;

its dregs have been consumed, because You were faithful.

Condemned before You take the stand,

Accusing eyes and palpable hatred surround You

And the wisdom of the ages is on the tip of Your tongue.

Echoes from eternity could fiercely consume each and every ugly lie that gathers, rages against You.

Every false witness condemns You as deserving of death.

But because You are faithful, to me,

You remain silent before Your shearers.

Your word spoke exploding volcanoes and thundering waterfalls into being,

And yet, here, when You could defend Yourself, You stay silent.

Because You are faithful

    Because You are just.

Thank You loving Father, that when we confess our sins, You forgive them. You have been faithful to us when we abandoned You. You have made a way to justify sinners. Thank You for Jesus, who stayed silent when He was accused so that His blood might cry out for my freedom. Help me to rejoice more in Your forgiveness, and in the relationship it has made possible with You. For Your name's sake, Amen.

Here is love, vast as the ocean,
Loving kindness, as the flood,
When the Prince of life, our ransom
Shed for us His precious blood.
Who His love will not remember?
Who can cease to sing His praise?
He will never be forgotten,
Throughout heaven's eternal days!
William Rees (1802–1883)

HE GIVES US MORE GRACE

JAMES 4:6

I say, 'Lord, I will give You all my praise.' On Sundays –
at least, during the singing…
during the good bits of the sermon.
I will give You half an hour each morning, apart from on busy
weekends.
On days when I am tired, too: then it might be less. But I will
usually give You that full half hour apart from when stress,
distractions, planning and to-do lists interrupt.
I will give You my money, reluctantly.
I will consider it all Yours
until I see something that I really (am sure I) need.
I will give You the last say,
apart from when I give You no say at all.
I will give You my future.
For about two minutes, as long as it looks bright.
Then I will grumble about my present and give You bitterness,
doubt, darkness, and despair, even in the face of remarkable
reasons for hope, and gratitude.

I will give You love or, at least,

I will give You excuses for my lack of love.

I will give You deceitful motives,

selfishness, destructive words, self-pity and despair. I will give You countless reasons to condemn me.

And when I give You apologies, and my most sincere repentance – I know – I will give You filthy rags.

Then You, looking right at me, in my shame, and shortcomings and grim and blatant nakedness, say:

'I will give you a clean slate.

I will give you great and precious promises.

I will give you My Son. And I will give you rest.

I will give you a righteousness that is not your own, but Mine.

I will give you a new life, a new heart, a new spirit, a new future.

I will give you a Redeemer,

I will give you hope, and a refuge; a strong tower.

I will give you an inheritance that can never perish, spoil or fade. I will give you power enough for perseverance.

And then I will reward you for having persevered. I will give you the right to become My child.

I will give you everything you need to approach My throne with boldness.

I will give you comfort, peace, joy and grace and grace and grace.'

Generous God, thank You for all the ways Your grace has overflowed to me. Thank You that the gospel is not what I can give You, but what You have given me!

Amazing grace, how sweet the sound,
That saved a wretch like me!
I once was lost, but now I'm found,
Was blind, but now I see.

Through many dangers, toils, and snares,
I have already come;
'Tis grace that brought me safe thus far,
And grace will lead me home!
John Newton (1725–1807)

I MAKE ALL THINGS NEW

REVELATION 21:5 (KJV)

S ometimes my biggest fear for the future is: what if nothing changes? The fight to be better, the fight against futility just seems too much. I fear: what if everything just stays the same? But into my fear, Jesus speaks and says: I make all things new.

Eden's Adam was asked to cultivate the Earth, to farm and tend it into something fruitful and productive and rich. But he failed. His legacy is a legacy of death. His world is in tatters and all its inhabitants feel the choke of the thorns and the triumph of the weeds. We look to the future and the only certainty we know is death.

But, hallelujah, the second Adam says, 'I make all things new.'

Jesus, the ultimate Gardener, is at work in the garden, and He comes to restore. All of the inevitabilities and heartaches of life in Adam's death-ridden garden will be redeemed, revived, rejuvenated. The biblical pattern for restoration is generous and glorious: where death has reigned, life will!

Jesus is the firstborn of the new creation; He's the guarantee that the broken world is being bound up and put right; He Himself is the evidence that all things are being made new.

When Mary was weeping in the garden, and thought she was talking to the gardener: she was! She saw Jesus, the new and better Adam, who came to make a world that's vibrant and bountiful. But she also saw in Him the first fruits of this creation, a physical reason to believe in all things made new.

There will be days where I may feel discouraged because I feel so much like the ground is hard, work feels futile, and death seems inevitable.

But the Risen Jesus makes secure this promise: He will bear fruit. And day by day, I get closer to a new heavens and a new earth.

And one day, I will meet that Gardener, whose hands are messy from His toil but whose heart is full of joy; He will welcome me into a world where all things are made new.

Thank You, my Father and my Redeemer, for Jesus, the second Adam. Thank You that He is at work to redeem the world, and to redeem the brokenness in my life too. Give me faith in that promise today –that You are making all things new, including me. For Your glory, Amen.

No more let sins and sorrows grow,
Nor thorns infest the ground;
He comes to make His blessings flow
Far as the curse is found.
Isaac Watts (1674–1748)

SURELY I AM COMING SOON

REVELATION 22:20 (ESV)

I cannot think of more comforting words than these words from the Lord Jesus at the end of Revelation. We live with a world that is groaning in pain, groaning as it waits for the birth of something new, and glorious. We long for this birthday! And as we long for it, we're not just looking forward to the day when Jesus returns, when death and all its friends are swallowed up in victory, but for every day afterwards too. When He reigns in perfect righteousness and justice. When every tear is wiped away. When the earth as it was intended is enjoyed as it was intended: vibrant with colour and life and grace and gratitude and glory!

His promise to us is that this day is coming soon.

To the darkness;
To nights of bloodshed and of wailing,
To the shrill cries of victory from the mouths of merciless slaughterers;
He is coming soon.

147

To the murkiest of perversions that have long lurked in the shadow,
To presumptions that threats might hold the power to conceal,
To all that has soiled innocence, trampled life, extinguished hope;
He is coming soon.
To brutality;
To violence;
To arrogant, aggressive minds;
To tyranny in cities, and in homes and minds and bedrooms;
To meaningless religiosity and empty masks of morality;
To staggering pomposity that would patronize the truth;
To stubbornness and cynicism and damaging indifference;
To prejudice, to selfishness, to unashamed egotism;
To judgments laid heavy without meekness, without truth;
To devastating foolishness wrapped in words of empty wisdom;
To clanging gongs and echoes; to every kind of lovelessness;
To tombs; to graves; to every evil power;
He is coming for His victory, and He is coming soon (Rev. 1:7; 22:7).

Lord Jesus, risen, conquering Son. Thank You that You are not a trite answer to the galling questions of life. You have suffered violence and death and the worst of humanity. You are the Lamb who was slain; You are sufficient for the depths of darkness; You are the light that cannot be overcome. Thank You for Your promise that is our hope and happiness, our source of peace and patience: You are coming soon. Yes, Lord – come soon! Amen.

When Christ shall come, with shout of acclamation,
And lead me home, what joy shall fill my heart!
Then I shall bow with humble adoration
And there proclaim, 'My God, how great Thou art!'
Carl Boberg (1859–1940) & Stuart K. Hine (1899–1989)

APPENDICES

APPENDIX 1:
BITE-SIZED ADVICE FOR FRIENDS OF THE DEPRESSED

APPENDIX 2:
BITE-SIZED ADVICE FOR DEPRESSED DAYS

APPENDIX 3:
DEAR DEPRESSION

APPENDIX 4:
WHEN IT'S TOO DARK EVEN FOR BITE-SIZED BIBLE

APPENDIX 1:

BITE-SIZED ADVICE FOR FRIENDS OF THE DEPRESSED

F ew of these ideas are mine; they are just a record of some of what my family and friends did for me during my more wintery seasons. These people embodied this amazing verse from 1 Samuel 23:16: 'Jonathan went to David at Horesh and helped him to find strength in God.' I am so thankful for their friendship; their love, self-sacrifice and forgiveness. They have been a reminder of God's kindness. Sometimes I saw it on the darkest of days, sometimes only when the sun came out.

SPEAK. Say words to your depressed friend. If you don't say it, they will be assuming things, without even realising assumptions are being made. Generally speaking, these assumptions will not be good. Tell them the truth: if they are being a pain, you can say that. But if they're not, reassure them: you are loved, you are valued, you are fun! Or how you are being now is not the quintessential you! Better still: write it down. Give them tangible words they can hold on to and read and reread when condemnation is whirring through their heads.

INVITE and insist! If you invite your friend to do something, and they say no, ask again. Or at least, tell them they will be missed – that it won't be the same without them. Encourage them to make a mind decision rather than a feelings decision. Do what you can to make it easier for them: 'Let's meet and go together'; 'Let's get ready together'; get to the venue first; tell them who else is expected so that they can prepare. This insistence on their presence is not to torture them, but to encourage them to stimulate their minds with something other than... their minds. Although it doesn't always feel like it, real world data can be a friend to the depressed mind.

RECOGNIZE the small steps: Be aware that being out is difficult: let them know you know that. They might need to go home. Congratulate them on making it out!

FEED them well. Most depressed people have a complex relationship with food. But if you can share meat and two veg with them from time to time, they will be comforted by health and normality. Eating well helps, but it's extremely hard to organize when you are depressed.

BE THERE. You probably can't offer solutions, and it's often better if you don't. Either the cause of depression is impossible to access, or it feels like the last ten, fifteen years have all led to this valley. There's a whole lifetime of narrative that is making this moment unbearable – and you probably won't be able to unpick it or solve it. But you can make the most present moment better.

ADMIT the complexity. You will desperately, desperately want to take the pain away. You will at times want to shake your friend, slap your friend, shout your friend out of their way of seeing things. Avoid doing these things; be kind and be there. Tell them how frustrated you are and how you wish the darkness could be swallowed up now. Let your anger fuel your prayer. Don't be afraid to admit the depths of the darkness: the problem does not have to be denied or simplified or untangled for Jesus to be able to redeem it. Gloriously, He can plumb the bitter depths, and work there – in the valley of shadows – for good.

CALL OUT the sickness! Of course there will be sin in your friend, as there is in us all. But it will help if you know and talk distinctly about the symptoms of depression. Your friend will want to put all the blame on themselves but they will need you to identify the symptoms at work. Be informed about the sickness and the symptoms, and be willing to take your friend to a doctor or counsellor.

SHARE! Your depressed friend is still your friend: let them know what you need prayer for, where your difficulties are. This is a gentle reminder that there is life outside the depressed mind and that gasps of freedom can come in loving others. It also reassures them that your relationship is a friendship, rather than your being a person and their being a sack of (very heavy, very sad) stones.

BE THEIR PERSPECTIVE: Let them ask you: 'This is how I see it – is this right?' Sometimes they will take what you say on board. Some things will be impossible for them to compute. But later, they might remember what you've said. Especially if you wrote it down!

FORGIVE them. They will let you down. They will be afraid. They will doubt your friendship. They will not find things fun that they should find fun. They will be defensive – and offensive. The kindest thing you can do for them is to forgive them. If they hurt you, tell them – explain why you are hurt. They may apologize, or they may be blind. Try to forgive them anyway.

TELL them you are sad that they are sad. If you don't know what else to say, say this. It will make an enormous difference and is infinitely better than saying nothing.

PRAY. Depression is painful. And lonely. And destructive. It is, put simply, your mind telling you things that aren't true. Pray that the truth gets through. Pray for flashes of hope, waves of hope, torrents of hope. Remind your friend that their darkness is temporary – even if it lasts a lifetime. Pray that the darkness lifts soon. I have found prayers that depression goes away so helpful: it acknowledges that depression is awful, that we are powerless to do anything about it, but that we rely on a God who is able. Maybe He won't heal, but it helps me to remember that He can. And it's good for all of us to remember that there are some problems we can't fix. Let that drive us to the One who can make a difference.

APPENDIX 2:

BITE-SIZED ADVICE FOR DEPRESSED DAYS

IT'S COMPLEX! Many people will offer you 'golden bullet' suggestions, but allow yourself the truth: it's hard, it sucks, and there aren't any easy solutions. These are suggestions that might help, but some days depression feels too strong. Read Appendix 3: He will do good anyway.

GO TO THINGS YOU DON'T WANT TO GO TO. Planning your weekend? Or your holiday? What you will feel like doing is nothing. So try to plan with your head rather than your instinctive feelings about it. Plan with the facts of: 'Where there are people there is reality', 'My mind alone is not good company right now' and 'My friends are my friends'.

TRY TO ENJOY THE TEENIEST OF THINGS, even if it's just for that moment. Sitting in the sun's warmth? Cherish that goodness. Have time for a cup of tea? Enjoy each sip.

DOWNSIZE YOUR EXPECTATIONS. What you are enduring is hard! Did you eat fruit today? Achievement. Did you exercise? Achievement. Did you go to something you did not want to go to? Achievement. Did you stop yourself from knocking out that person who asked you why you were sad when the Bible says be joyful? Achievement. In fact, you get double for that.

USE THE ENERGY SPURTS YOU HAVE to love people. Pray, when you can, that God will help you with this – and that He will use you even when you're unaware of it.

INTERRUPT THE 'AIRTIME' of the dark thoughts. Listen to music to drown them out (I found bass-heavy headphones worked most effectively), and inhabit the lyrics. If the lyrics are too much like the harsh hissing of your mind, find something else to listen to. Read books with short chapters – and big yourself up chapter by chapter. Watch TV that makes you laugh: things like *Mock the Week* or *8 Out of 10 Cats* are better than more emo-heavy sitcoms.

READ THE PSALMS. Even if it's just a few verses a day – even if it's Psalm 88 every day for many, many days.

CALL OUT THE DEPRESSION, and try to laugh at it. Try and see the funny side of yourself – and once you know what the symptoms are, try laughing at them. Try laughing at your mind's amazing way of making everything about you. Of blaming everything on you. Of reading your failure into every situation imaginable. There are probably some things that have happened that are not your fault(!). Depression can be outrageous and, occasionally, you might be able to find it hilarious. This won't always be possible – but it's worth a try.

TRY TO TRUST YOUR FRIENDS. If your friends are your friends, then they may rightly tell you that what you currently believe about yourself is not true. When they tell you this, remember that you can trust them. They are your friends; what they are saying is more trustworthy than what your mind is currently shouting at you.

REMEMBER: the cross is atonement enough. Jesus shed His blood for you, He suffered for you, He felt shame for you and was destroyed for you. There will be dark times when you may want to hurt yourself or cause yourself to suffer because you feel so ashamed, so desperate and so sad. But the cross is atonement enough. It is atonement enough.

Remember Jesus – without trying to find a connection to you. Jesus is powerful, Jesus is at work. Jesus is reigning. Jesus is humble. Jesus is generous. Jesus is kind. Jesus loves the poor. Jesus will come again. Jesus is bold. Jesus is a warrior. Jesus has the victory. The list could go on...

You might not be able to see any of this in connection to you right now, but rejoice in Him because of who He is.

HOLD ON TO THE PROMISE of the final day. Darkness will get swallowed up: even this darkness. This darkness will not be able to overcome the light of Christ. Oh that the night might give us joy in how glorious the morning will be! Try to see the depth of your pit as evidence of the power of Jesus to redeem. Even in this pit, this darkness, this gloom: He is with you. And the Morning Star will rise!

Find it impossible to believe or do any of the above?

BE ASSURED – He will do good anyway (see Appendix 4).

APPENDIX 3:

DEAR DEPRESSION

Dear Depression,

I can really only write you this letter because you're not currently around. When you are, it's very difficult to see you. It's very hard to see anything other than a blank of darkness, and you don't seem to be anything very separate from me. But while you're away, (feel free to stay away as long as possible), I thought I'd write.

So, dear depression.

I suppose in many ways 'dear' seems utterly inappropriate. You have not been kind to me, and to many others I know of, know and dearly love.

It took me years to recognize you. When you came up in conversation, you were so very good at drawing my attention to my own past, my own failures, my own sin, as explanations for the sadness you convinced me I deserved. You had me believe a whole host of things instead of believing I was depressed: that I was just especially bad, especially condemned, especially worthless, especially socially malfunctional.

When I first sought treatment you told me I was treating sin with medicine. But after the pills got you to pipe down a bit, I finally began to know something about you.

You've sat on my chest on countless mornings; you've been condemnation's megaphone; you've been an ugly neon sign pointing me in the direction of self-destruction and self-harm. You've known my weakness and you've wielded it against me; you've sharpened its blade. You've loaded my heart with sadness and taken hope captive. You've turned up uninvited and made nothing appealing to me but sleep.

I wish I never had to see you again, I wish your influence and reach was gone, because life is dark enough without your contributions.

But, dear depression, there are some things I think you should know.

When I was a teenager, and you told me that I was the worst human there was, when my dreams and thoughts were heavy with destruction, and when my thoughts were dark and landed in my conscience with pangs of horror and shame, when hurting myself seemed like the only option left, you took away every way for me. Except for Jesus.

Jesus became my way. You shut all the doors to freedom, but Jesus told me in the darkness: His blood was shed for mine. His blood was enough. Age 17, you made the cross even more beautiful to me – it was such a relief. You had me believing I was the worst of sinners, but Jesus said He came for the worst. You didn't bank on Jesus being sufficient for the worst of condemnations you brought – that even for the vilest, most self-absorbed, wretched girl, He might hold out forgiveness. But He did; Jesus became my way.

When I went to university, and you told me that I couldn't leave my room in halls without bringing shame on myself and the gospel, when it took me minutes and then hours to leave for a shower because I was so afraid of how I would mess up, when I believed you, and so gave up on freedom and parties and friendships and showers when I needed them, you took away every hope I had of justification. Except for Jesus.

Jesus was my justification. You blocked off my joy and life, but Jesus told me in the darkness: God is the One who justifies. He was my justification. Aged 20, you made the cross even more beautiful to me – I was acutely aware of everything I wasn't, and it made Jesus, standing in my place, my only hope.

When two years of ministry in France had left me feeling stripped of everything, and you told me that my hopes for ministry were ashes, that I was friendless and hopeless and fruitless, when my identity felt like rubble, and you told me I was inadequate, insufficient, stupid, and I believed I was spiritually barren, Jesus was my righteousness.

Time and time again you jumped on the band-wagon of my sin and my weakness and used it to say: 'No way forward. You are cursed.' But Jesus told me in the darkness: I became a curse for you. He said, whatever else is happening, it cannot be a curse. He showed me His scarred hands in the darkness.

And because you'd had me so convinced that I had nothing but wretchedness, the hands held out to me were beautiful because they were my only hope. I had no other refuge.

Depression, I don't blame you for everything. Of course, my sin would have me say, 'It's all your fault.' And you would have me believe it's all sin's fault.

But the faithful grace of Jesus means that, ultimately, it doesn't matter – because in my sin, and in you, my depression, He's been working, and He will be working, relentlessly, for good. You have influenced my life greatly, but you're a speck compared to Jesus. And where you have changed my life, where I've felt most broken, most hopeless, you've sent me running to the arms of Jesus. You have made the gospel sweet to me. If I had never known you, but for not knowing you I would have known Jesus less, then I would choose to know you all over again.

So, dear depression.

I am grateful for the times you've been a friend to grace; you've 'driven me from the paths of ease, to storm the secret place .'

That said, I won't miss you when you're gone. And you will be, completely, one day soon.

APPENDIX 4:

WHEN IT'S TOO DARK EVEN FOR BITE-SIZED BIBLE

I don't want to do today.

I wake up and immediately want to be asleep again; I want to crawl back to the comfort of unconsciousness, where I'm safe from the steady waves of anxiety, anger, disappointment, shame, breaking over my waking mind.

I want to forget. The past feels like a fully-stocked weaponry for shame: that's where the trying happened, and the failing happened. The past is heavy with disappointment and its weight seeps into my view of the future. Fear that trying again might mean failing again eats away at hope. And so the present is burdened with frustration: I feel paralysed, inadequate, sad.

I want to forget.

I should get out of bed, get dressed, call someone. But I can't think who to call, I can't decide what to wear, and I really don't want to get out of bed.

Instead, I want to forget. Get my binge watching on. Go back to sleep. Get a multi-pack of something sugar-loaded and eat until the despair subsides.

But somehow I know I need to not forget.

I desperately, in the manner of someone gasping for breath, need to remember the Lord.

Remember that: God has spoken to us, that the Lord Himself will provide, that He is faithful and just, that He has seen my tears, that He Himself is my peace…

Each is glorious alone. I see them from a distance and know – if I could just get a grip on one of them, I might be able to get out of bed.

But what if I can't? Or don't? Or won't?

The good news, the big relief and my only real hope is that whether I remember the truth about God this morning or not,

THE LORD WILL DO GOOD ANYWAY.

He will reign in robust goodness and generous kindness and sovereign providence anyway. Right in the shadows where my anxiety lurks, my doubt clouds Him out, right in the pit where the past is a barrage of shame and the future is a wall of impossibilities:

THE LORD WILL DO GOOD ANYWAY.

When I was dead in my sins and His enemy – without the will or power to grasp it, Jesus was battling for me on the front line; plunging Himself into darkness; aligning Himself with my weakness and sin and unbelief; absorbing the full penalty for it all willingly; plumbing the depths so that no stone of my redemption was left unturned. When I was far off, blind, dead... He was coming out of the grave as a Victor for my sake.

And that could turn the tide.

Whether I can grasp it this morning or not, He is still the ordainer of my days, He is still my present help, He is still the guarantee of my forgiveness, my most loyal companion, the lover of my bruised soul, and He is still reigning as Victor.

This morning, I am no victor.

I feel utterly defeated. I am weak and faithless and doubt-filled and afraid, and I don't want to do today.

BUT HE WILL DO GOOD ANYWAY.

ACKNOWLEDGEMENTS

To write a book about suffering, you don't just need friends who support you as you write (which is an enormous ask in itself), but friends who support you in your suffering. There are too many to mention here, but I am thankful for every one.

To say that this book would not exist without Hugh and Grace Barne would not be an exaggeration: thank you for your work of faith, labours of love, and patience of hope. This book exists because of you!

Thank you to Catherine Weston who has not only been a friend through all kinds of thick and thin, but who also encouraged me to write. You were the midwife for *A Certain Brightness*.

Thank you to all the supporters of the blog. Writing can be isolating, so I am thankful for engaged readers who took the time to say where it had made a difference.

Thank you for the whole team at Christian Focus, who understood the vision for the devotions and ran with it – the book they've delivered is more than I could have imagined. Thank you to Rosanna for being such a generous and efficient editorial manager, to Helen for her thoughtfully suggested edits, and to Rebekah for such striking illustrations. Thank you to Peter and James for taking on board my opinions on the cover. I know there were a lot of them!

Enormous thanks to Jane Williams for proofreading the initial manuscript and for always keeping me in good supply of flowers.

Thank you to my pal Katie Stileman for being a wonderful reminder of the faithfulness of Jesus: I could have done very little this past year without you. Or Folklore.

I'm so thankful to my family, in Cardiff and in Canada, who have lived by my side, through my depression, and through my writing, and sometimes through both of them operating at the same time, with a side serving of year 8. Thank you. As well as everything else, thank you for making me laugh every day; could there be a more robust reminder of the goodness of God?

Biggest thanks to Jesus – the source of every other blessing, and the most certain Brightness. 'No one whose hope is in you will ever be put to shame' (Ps. 25:3).

Christian Focus Publications

Our mission statement —

STAYING FAITHFUL

In dependence upon God we seek to impact the world through literature faithful to His infallible Word, the Bible. Our aim is to ensure that the Lord Jesus Christ is presented as the only hope to obtain forgiveness of sin, live a useful life and look forward to heaven with Him.

Our books are published in four imprints:

CHRISTIAN
FOCUS

Popular works including biographies, commentaries, basic doctrine and Christian living.

CHRISTIAN
HERITAGE

Books representing some of the best material from the rich heritage of the church.

MENTOR

Books written at a level suitable for Bible College and seminary students, pastors, and other serious readers. The imprint includes commentaries, doctrinal studies, examination of current issues and church history.

CF4•K

Children's books for quality Bible teaching and for all age groups: Sunday school curriculum, puzzle and activity books; personal and family devotional titles, biographies and inspirational stories — because you are never too young to know Jesus!

Christian Focus Publications Ltd,
Geanies House, Fearn, Ross-shire,
IV20 1TW, Scotland, United Kingdom.
www.christianfocus.com